MY LIFE CONFUSED

Somebody light a candle to dispel the darkness

A step-by-step guide to help you navigate life

First published by LAUREN MOOI Publishing

First Edition January 2025 paperback

ISBN: 978-1-0370-4367-3

www.laurenmooipublishing.com

MY LIFE CONFUSED

Somebody light a candle to dispel the darkness

A step-by-step guide to help you navigate life

By

Sunil Osman

Table of Contents

Dedication

This book is dedicated to every soul that I have interacted with during my life's journey up to this point. Every single, event, every single moment I have had on this earthly plane has given me the strength to grow as a spiritual being.

The people who are blessed to read my book will understand that we are spiritual beings having a human experience.

Love, Light and Peace.

Keep smiling and just be happy. #sunnymotiv

FACULTY OF HUMANITIES

2/9/2021

Testimonial: Sunny Motiv Vol 1

Amidst the throws of 2020 and the COVID-19 pandemic, I came across a ray of light in the form of Sunny Motiv. The year was indeed unprecedented, with the national lockdown leaving us feeling isolated despite online lecturing and digital 'socials'. For me personally, a PhD needed completion while I was adapting to our new normal way of life.

I discovered Sunil on social media, when anxiety interrupted my sleep one night. This anxiety arose from own studies and the fact that my students were scattered all over the country, with some really struggling to adapt to online learning. What initially struck me about Sunil was his overwhelming positivity. So naturally, I was thrilled when I had heard that he had authored a book.

In the final months of my PhD, Sunny Motiv encouraged me in extraordinary ways. One of my favorite quotes, pertinent to the world at present is "***No matter what your surroundings may be, never forget your potential***". Waking up to a positive thought every morning helped to curb my anxiety and motivated me to work harder despite the uncertainty in the world around me. On every page of Sunny Motiv too, Sunil's amazing personality and warmth is evident.

In 2021, I will be sharing copies of Sunny Motiv with some of my students, in hope that they too will be inspired.

Warm regards,

Ms. Jacqueline Moodley
Lecturer
Department of Psychology

Introduction

We all have experiences which shape our lives differently and we either learn something from it or run from it. My life is a colourful mixture of both. Sometimes the weight of the world can pull you down into a pit of darkness, disbelief and hopelessness. And other times it feels like there is no weight. While we welcome these times, we also know that something is wrong and needs to change through acceptance or surrendering. This is my life confused.

SUNNYMOTIV is the first book I wrote and it was inspired by my life experiences. This book explains those experiences in more detail. We don't face life alone, especially when we think we do. Our circumstances may be different, but there are always life lessons which shape us.

Instructions

This book was written to help you navigate through the confusion life brings in a society where instant gratification and the pursuit of perfection seems to be the order of the day. Here you will learn how to pick up on queues, such as "That person isn't right for you," or "The job you want isn't the one you need," or "Do you know why you are here?" Understanding who you are is only the beginning to living a purpose filled life.

What you will need;

1. Journal or notebook
2. Pen or pencil (different colours)
3. Paper (that you don't mind throwing away later if you need to)
4. Sticky notes (optional)
5. Scrap book items (optional)
6. An open mind and willingness to put pride and ego aside while you learn and unlearn
7. Copy of SUNNYMOTIV (optional but recommended)

Day 1 – The beginning

I was born in 1982, on December 10th to a lovely couple commonly known as my parents. We moved around quite a bit growing up. Between Cape Town, Johannesburg, and Pretoria in South Africa, it wasn't easy, but I experienced more than the average kid and I'm grateful for it today.

I got my first degree in Politics, Public Administration and Gender Studies at the University of Cape Town and my Honors in Public Policy at the same tertiary institution. When I did my Honours, my thesis was based on Post Apartheid Woman Empowerment in Local Government. I worked for National Government for quite some time and yet I still felt empty. I reflected on this emptiness and realised I found happiness from the time I was knee high to a grasshopper, doing things on stage as an actor, singer and speaker. I then reflected moved back into acting, hosting radio shows again and being a MC as a profession, while even dabbling in on the South African Comedy circuit for 9 years. This is where I found my calling. With every opportunity the entertainment industry had to offer, I made sure that I thrived. It started as a dream and continues to be my evolving reality.

In my first book SUNNYMOTIV, one of the quotes I explained is "Your dreams can take you anywhere and everywhere if you let them." Why do we dream? Is it because a dream allows you to be anything you want? Or is it because dreams come true? Have you ever considered that dreams are only but a vision of what your reality is capable of becoming? Well, it's true. Your dreams may invite the idea that allows you to be anything you want, but it is you who will make it possible. You see, dreams are like a short movie trailer. There's only enough to entice you, which leaves you wanting to know more. But sadly, that's all your dream can offer. If you want to know how the movie ends, you have to buy the ticket. The first step to living out your dreams is realizing that you actually want whatever you're dreaming of more than anything else in the world. The second step is knowing where to begin. The how will follow after. You see, many times we stop ourselves from achieving greatness because we don't know where to begin. Because we are so worried about the how, we lose sight of the now. What can I do now? How do you eat an elephant? One small bite at a time. The giant looking obstacle in front of you isn't what's holding you back, it's the doubt that has taken residence within your mind. Somewhere along the line, you have told yourself that you are not worthy. You are not capable. You are not ready or you are not deserving. All these things are lies. The dreams you have for yourself was placed inside of you for a reason. Instead of looking at the obstacle as that, let's rather change it into a challenge by saying; you are worthy, you are capable, you are ready and you are deserving. Challenges are things that make you great, it is opportunities that will test your endurance, your mind and capabilities. When you say yes to something, you have accepted the challenge. But when you say no, you have created an obstacle. The one thing I love about dreaming, is the fact that you already have the idea on how to achieve it, because you wouldn't be dreaming of it if you didn't know what to do next. So, let's start somewhere.

Find a comfortable, quiet space where you can be alone with your thoughts. Think about all the dreams you had growing up as a child. Go back and look at when you first had that dream and then think about why. Open your journal and write down all the dreams you had as a child. Use colour pens or pencils, making it more personal. Notice how you feel about it as you write. Feel it and take your mind back there before you were socially conditioned.

Now think about all the dreams or just one at a time, that you have as an adult. Understand why you have this dream and write the reasons and feelings down. Notice how it makes you feel, and write that down too.

You may notice an overlap between your childhood dreams and now. Some may still be there and others may not. What you may also notice is the ones that have crossed over may have a different meaning, same concept. For example; you want to help people. As a child you thought becoming a teacher is the only way to help people. But as an adult, you realize that becoming a psychologist is a better way to help. Remember, just because your dreams have changed, doesn't mean that you've let yourself down or that you're a failure. All it means is that you are evolving into the person you were created to be.

Journal Notes

Day 2 – Potential

My parents divorced before my twenty-first birthday and I will admit that I was more relieved than I was sad. They are wonderful people, just separately. They no longer worked well as team and could only function in a healthy way, separated. Not many people who have experienced divorce can understand this concept. No matter how old you are. If your parents separate it's always a case of, *they no longer love me if they don't love each other*. Some children believe they are the reason why their parents are separating, even if the idea is far from the truth.

No matter what your surroundings may be, never forget your potential. Understanding how important this is, takes time and experience. No matter what happens around you, whether it may affect you directly or indirectly, do not forget who you are in all the pain. I know it's a difficult thing to comprehend. The exercise below may offer some assistance.

Vividly visualize a rosebud on a stem and then add another stem with a rosebud that has just bloomed next to it. Now add very green yet tattered leaves that have been eaten by worms to both roses. Some people allow their surroundings or circumstances they have been brought up in, define who they are and where they will end up in life. But I say to you, do not allow that to be you. Visualize the two roses again. They both have leaves around them that have been eaten away. These roses were both buds at the same time, but the one bloomed despite its surroundings and eaten leaves. Now are you going to be the rosebud that remains closed or are you going to be the rosebud that opens up all its glory despite its surroundings? Even though both rosebuds grew from the same soil and received the same attention and neglect, the one flourishes as the other shies away. It's mainly about being patient with yourself in achieving your full potential. Never let your surroundings overwhelm you. Be the rose that blooms no matter what.

Another way to look at it is the story of the wolf. One is revenge and the other is forgiveness. The one that you feed the most is the one that will grow up to be big and strong. Think about that again. Try it with other scenarios; one wolf is love and the other is hate. Which one will you feed? One wolf is faith and the other is fear. Which one will grow bigger and stronger in your life?
How many times have you just felt terribly down? Or everything you do or choose turns out SO negatively? Instead of allowing that negative outcome to consume you, rather choose to allow it to empower you. I'm talking about creating positivity in your life. This is one thing that is a lot easier said than done. One of the most

difficult things to do is think positively in a negative situation. Positivity is a state of mind. Thus, anyone can choose to tap into that state, at any given time. It is the ability to think differently when in a negative situation. The best way to create your own positivity is get rid of your negativity first.

How? You may ask. Simple. Go the way that the negative energy pushes you. If you feel like crying, then you should cry. If you feel like screaming, then you should go ahead and scream, preferably into a pillow, it's much more satisfying. And if you feel like breaking something then go on and break something, preferably nothing too expensive. But be sure to do all this in the privacy of your own home or bedroom. The last thing you need is someone saying that you can't express your negative emotions because that's a lie. You need to get rid of those feelings/thoughts/energy that is weighing you down, so that you can make room for all the positive. If it's just energy then surely it can be transferred somewhere else? Yes! Once the negative leaves you, you will not only start to feel better but you may also realize that everything which has gone wrong, has passed and you are now in a position to look forward to the good things that are coming your way. You will be able to see it, because positivity happens naturally when you make room for it. It is easier to tell yourself over and over that you can do something then to tell yourself that you can't.

The problem is believing in it. We tend to not believe in ourselves because we associate it with negative thoughts. Such as; conceitedness, self-centeredness, boastfulness and so on. Believing that you can do something is for you, not anyone else. When you start doing things to please others, that's when it becomes negative. As selfish as it may come across; stay on course and focus only on your future.

Your destiny is larger than you would like to believe. Don't allow what you think your destiny is, to limit you because your divine plan could be bigger than you may ever imagine. If you have a burning desire to be more than what you are now, do not let your circumstances or surroundings stop you from believing that you are worth more. Keep pushing to achieve those goals and never take your eye off that desire to be more. You will become what your destiny says you will be, as long as you don't give up. Once you have achieved your first set of goals, I encourage you to create new goals and also change paths. You will realize that the destiny you may have envisioned originally becomes completely different. This is all part of life's journey. Embrace it. Many believe that no matter the path you choose, your destiny will always fall into place. It's what you do with that information that will determine the best outcome for you.

What is your destiny and what path have you chosen? Like a tree of destiny which grows taller, each branch has its own leaves.

Journal Notes

Day 3 – Heartache, pain, trauma

I was about six years old when I experienced my first heartache. Her name was Maxine and she was my first kiss and safe space, since I had no idea what a crush was. We were best friends who had a normal loving experience until she told me that I could no longer play with her and the other kids because I was "too fat.". I had no idea what to expect after that. Every emotion I felt overwhelmed me. I couldn't help but feel as though I did something wrong, and I wanted to fix it. Not realizing that what I experienced was rejection. And from that moment on I started to develop a concern for other people's needs over and above my own.

A year after that I experienced trauma that a seven-year-old should never have to. I would visit my grandmother's house quite often and a certain family member would be there. When it was time for bed, this family member would make sure that he is lying next to me on my bed. He would then proceed to touch and kiss me inappropriately. It took me a short while to realize that what he was doing to me was wrong. That uncomfortable, gut feeling that we all have to warn us of trouble such as this, I had that all night. For a seven-year-old it was difficult to comprehend, but I somehow knew it was wrong. This went on for a few years. I never did anything about it because firstly, who would believe me? And secondly, I didn't want to upset him or disappoint him. My need to please people grew from that moment. One thing is for sure, this kind of trauma affected me later on in life. Especially when it happened again a few years later with a close friend of my brother's. I was in my early teens, and we would play fight. This friend was open about his sexuality and he insisted we play physical games such as wrestling. This was a manipulation tactic the friend used to get something out of it. The manipulation worked so well to a point where the roles reversed and the games became an expectation every time he visited. Eventually, I was the one who insisted on playing games. My brother was asleep when his friend manipulated me into thinking that this is something I wanted to do and that it was okay to do it with him. I developed a sense of disgust for all the moments it felt good. Not realizing at the time, that it was also known as guilt or shame. Although, I felt more shame than guilt since my "good feelings" were because of a boy and I knew that I was straight. There was no physical attraction, so why would there be any good feelings from the physical attention? I only realized years later that it was my desire I developed, to satisfy another person's needs before my own. I was manipulated into doing things that people wanted me to do to please them, and I allowed it. This went on for three or four years before coming to an end.

When I turned fifteen years old, I met a girl who I fell madly in love with. Also known as puppy dog love or young love. Her name was Jennifer. She was my first girlfriend, first time and first teenage love. The relationship was perfect up to the point where she cheated on me. Her actions broke my heart entirely, and of course I wondered what I could have done differently. Over the years I dated many beautiful women and all these relationships ended because I was not what they needed long term. It is a hard pill to swallow, but a very valuable lesson to learn. It was through these relationship experiences that confirmed my gift as a Healer. I also realized that when you try to make someone happy and they just never are, it's not your fault. Happiness comes from within, don't forget about yours. You cannot force happiness into a space where it is not accepted. Happiness is a state of mind. You can choose certain things to bring you happiness. Like ice-cream, or a comedy show or good company after a long day's work. Once you have decided on the things that make you happy, you will never lose it. People make the mistake by thinking someone else can bring them happiness, that is incorrect. Someone else can add to your joy but your happiness depends solely on you. For example, in relationships, too often one partner tries everything deemed possible to bring the other happiness, but it never works. This could be one of two reasons. The partner receiving the "happiness" may not recognise it has something that they decided on what makes them happy, or the one bringing the happiness may be the one who is actually not happy at all. Never expect your partner to make you happy if you never told them how to. Also, don't blame the other for not being happy after everything you have done, because it definitely isn't you. It might be their situation that is making them unhappy. Rather encourage them to go and do what makes them happy and ask them if you can join them. For example, a dancing class, painting or even just a social outing. You never know, their happy place might just become yours.

What brings you happiness?

Journal Notes

Day 4 – Try something new

After a massive change happens, there's a shift in mindset and character. Every time we experience something life changing, no matter how small or big, there's always a lesson in it. The reason why we continuously experience trials is so that we can grow as the person we're evolving into. There was a time when I worked on a cruise ship, and I realized for the first time what loneliness is. Extreme loneliness. I put myself in that situation to find myself, and since then I never felt lonely again. It is in that moment, I realized I only had two people in my life that I could count on, and one of those people was me. That's when I realized how important self-love is. For many years I put everyone else above myself and forgot how to be treated. My first self-love journey started in 1994 when I had my first reiki session. And the reiki practitioner actually said to me, "One day you may do reiki." I never acknowledged what she said, but over time I started seeing things that was not evident to others. I'm not talking about paranormal things; I'm referring to energies. I would have high energy experiences and then drop when societal norms take over. This happened a lot throughout the years. Thankfully I don't do that anymore. I am fully embraced in who I am, with a full understanding of what that means. I know this is my life's purpose, a healer. I'm not doing this because I have to, I'm doing this because I want to. I took this interest a bit further and became a Reiki practitioner. I then

progressed to Master level and I am currently a Master Usui Reiki Practitioner. I have never been happier.
The first thing I realized going through my journey of change and transformation, is that I don't need anyone to get me there. Understanding that outside validation isn't always a positive thing and for your personal growth it's not necessary at all. The opinions of others should not affect the trajectory of your life. It's not about being on your own, it's about being an individual. And knowing that you don't have to satisfy all the needs of someone else, they are just as responsible for their happiness as you are for yours.

One way to achieve this goal for yourself is to try something new every day.

To learn something new every day is about growing as an individual. Whatever is being learnt should be something significant enough to contribute to your mental and spiritual growth. Decide every day on what you would like to learn. Whether it is a new recipe you saw online, or a game that you can play with your family or even just something to add to your general knowledge bank. Make an effort to learn how to do it, and then just do it. You could also decide on something long term and fun, like taking dance lessons by yourself or with your partner. The possibilities are endless, and the human mind will only grow as far as you will allow it. Don't limit yourself in a limitless world. Learning something new every day is also about learning about you. Discovering who you are and what makes you tick is crucial for spiritual growth and evolving. It may even allow you to impart knowledge to others and help them learn something new about themselves. Going a day without learning something new is a missed opportunity that you can never recreate.

Take a moment to decide on what you've always wanted to learn. Don't overthink it, and just write down the first thing that comes to mind. For the next week, research more on what you have chosen to learn. This will help you ease into it and not go full steam ahead, which will overwhelm you and inadvertently force you to quit before you ever starting. Pace yourself for your soul and sanity.

Give yourself five options to choose from.

Journal Notes

Day 5 – Positive thinking

For many years I was attracted to brokenness. Not realising that it was my own brokenness fuelling this attraction. The worst part of this situation was the attachments. When you find someone who can unknowingly fill that void inside of you, unexpected attachments occur. Many times, these attachments grew because of the bond we created caused by our idea of what love is. I am a hyoka empath and I tend to follow where my heart leads. I feel everyone's energy and their pain. I also feel as though it is my job to help them. On a few occasions, my feelings were wrong. This resulted in bad break ups, depression and suicidal thoughts and attempts. Sometimes, trusting your feelings isn't the best option. Feelings or emotions were never meant to turn into the driving force that leads you to greatness, because it is fleeting. Emotions are created by moments and as soon as it passes so does the emotion. If we allow the feelings to remain, we may end up concluding certain events based off on that one fleeting moment. Therefore, feelings cannot be trusted. But your heart and mind can.

Your mind can change your day in an instant. And because thoughts are logical, you can trust that it will remain constant for as long as you will it to be so. The first thing you can do is change your pattern of thinking by telling your brain to shut up. Too often we tend to think of the worst first. Whether we are aware of it or not. Our natural instinct is to prepare for the worst. The reason why we do this is for survival. Human beings are naturally programmed to think of the worst first, so that we can avoid it at all costs. Be it physical, mental, emotional or spiritual. Our first goal is to protect ourselves from anything and everything that may cause us harm. Now that that's out the way, let's start changing our thinking pattern by directing it in a positive way.

Build your positivity by starting your day with words that can help you set the platform for how your day may turn out. This is not just about saying words like, "I am positive." You have to believe it. Though it may come across as rather odd and cliched, when you truly believe in the words you speak to yourself, you will experience a mild shiver from within. You will have raised your vibrations and soon you will start to smile, because your faith in yourself has increased exponentially. That is the rise of chemical levels in the brain and with it the body reacts accordingly. In other words, you will start to feel good. Many have experienced goosebumps when doing this effectively, but if at first you don't DO NOT PLACE YOURSELF UNDER PRESSURE.

Today's task is simple. Write down three positive things that you believe and know for a fact about yourself. For example; I'm really good at baking.

Journal Notes

Day 6 – Positive affirmation

Start your day with positivity and the words I AM…

I cannot stress the importance of positivity, enough! Because we face a tremendous amount of negative energy every day, it is difficult to remain in that positive space. And unfortunately, we cannot escape the negativity around us. That is why we have to practice positive thinking. So, when you wake up in the morning, do not just say the words "I am…" believe in whatever you choose to follow as your words of encouragement for the day. Something simple like, "I am going to have a good day" and believing it can change your mindset. Try it. Believe it. Do It. This is about recognizing your capabilities, by not limiting yourself at the same time. Once this is achieved, remember to practice gratitude towards it.

Write down three I AM sentences and recite them until you believe what you're saying. Once that happens, you can then write down three more. Use your sticky notes for each I AM and place them where you can see it every day. For example, on your mirror or in your car or somewhere on your desk at work. You are already…

I am

I am

I am

Journal Notes

Day 7 – Positive energy will drive out the negative

Being in a positive state of mind requires a lot of energy and focus, so it is difficult to stay positive continuously. Especially while living in a world that has negative news reported every single day. Now you may not be able to escape it, but you can learn how to block it out or channel it into positive energy. Every time you hear something negative, ask yourself; does it affect you? How will it affect you? What impact will it have? And do you need to concern yourself with it right now? If you have answered no to all the questions above, then you will have no need to allow the negative to enter into your space. It will be difficult at first, but once you master the distinction, you will find that blocking negativity out will become like second nature, and the easiest thing to do. Always keep focusing on you, your family and your well-being to create continuous positive energy.

Think of negative energy as another form of lies. When you start telling yourself nothing but good things, negativity will appear as lies.

1. Describe your mood today. (One-word sentences are welcomed.)
2. Do you know why you're feeling this way?
3. Are you happy with your current mood? If no, would you like to change it?

If you answered yes to the second question, take three slow deep breathes in through your nose, hold it for a few seconds (not till you pass out) and out through your mouth. Repeat this until a level of calmness is felt. And smile. That's all you need to do right now, is smile. Keep smiling and just be happy #sunnymotiv

Journal Notes

Day 8 – Cancel the negative

Blocking out negativity

This is actually harder to do than most people would like to believe. I know we can be as positive as possible and change negative energy into positive energy. You might wonder how easy it can be to actually follow through and keep a constant positive state of mind. When you choose to embody a positive vibrational frequency, you will find that in some situations with negativity all round, you will be criticized, judged and forced to break your vibrational level down to a negative low level. The best thing to do, would be to surround yourself with positive situations, but this isn't always possible. Being aware of the negativity is the best approach here, so you can mentally and spiritually block it out. The results are amazing and you will see and feel the difference if done correctly. The shift will be evident in a way that your vibration increases. You may even find negative people or situations get attracted to you in order to try and drain your high vibration. Know when to just listen and not react. Protect your energy.

Day 9 – Encourage others

Never underestimate the positive energy and power in supporting one another. Life is tough already as it is. The last thing we need is to bring each other down. Most of the time it is done unknowingly and unintentionally. However, in that moment we do not see it as that. We see it as a willing participant. Someone who is willing to break down our spirits on purpose and for personal reasons. My life is not short of disappointments and betrayals from friends, colleagues and family. Instead of thinking that I need to get even or hold grudges, I simply just feel what I need to feel, move on and focus my energy where it is needed. The reward of helping or supporting others outweighs the pain of trying so hard to be accepted by the masses.

There is no greater pleasure in seeing people become successful because of something you have advised on or supported them with. We often forget to support each other because we are so consumed with our own lives. This is about giving back and also being a mentor to others. When you give support and guidance to help someone grow; you cannot help but trigger a surge of positive vibrations within them. I have heard the saying that "your success is my success." And as much as this may be true, it is also about fulfilling your own soul's purpose. Every person on earth will have their own life experience. Some people will grow up with role models, mentors and leaders, and others won't. Do not block those people who may need a little extra along the way, because we can all be healers. Make sure you give as much as you can without expecting anything in return. This is one of the greater things you can do to raise your vibrations.

Day 10 – Just do it

I had a relationship with a girl named Faye. And around the time that we met, I hadn't realized how much pain I was carrying with me. To the point where she would introduce me to drugs and I would be open to it. We bonded over the intoxicated feeling we got from doing drugs. My world of trouble disappeared as my body was pulled into a state of nonexistence. That's what it felt like at the time. I couldn't get enough of her or the drugs. Despite the fact that the come down was notably the worst thing to ever exist in this world, I was still drawn to her and the highs I got from doing drugs. Until it all came to a sudden halt and the relationship ended. I was devastated when I lost her, which led to depression. To combat that depression, I used drugs for five days straight, with the intent of overdosing. Thankfully I was not successful, because it didn't control me, but me it. Choices.

In moments like this, it is difficult to bounce back if you do not have the right support structure or understanding from people around you. It may be hard to believe, but the only person you depend on, at that time, is you. So, get up and do something. Even if it is just one thing. Get up and do it.

This is about completing a task to give yourself a sense of accomplishment and purpose. Every now and then we are consumed by the activities of our daily lives. We focus our energy on many duties. We ought to take each task one at a time, even if it means creating a list of priorities. We have to keep the world going round, because the world needs to be in constant rotation. The idea here is to do things and do them to the best of your ability. Too many times when we are consumed by responsibilities, we forget about completing the simplest things with diligence. Never neglect the simple details. Do your duties with sheer brilliance and also do not forget to acknowledge it once you are done. Praise yourself on a job well done when appropriate. Physically pat yourself on your back.

Think of one task that you are dying to get to. The task that frightens you because you have convinced yourself that you're no good at it. Write it down below or in your journal, along with a plan of action. The simpler the plan, the better the solution. Do not complicate it.

Journal Notes

Day 11 – You will get through it

Another time that caused a great depression in my life was when I found out that the woman I became really close with was no longer moving to South Africa. This devastated me because I had envisioned a future with her and made many efforts to stay in touch energetically and emotionally. Needless to say, I got through it after reflection and realisations of a one-sided distant relationship.

I wish I could say life is really all sunshine and rainbows. But unfortunately, it is not. We need thunder storms and rain to understand and appreciate the sunshine and rainbows. Not everything is set in black and white, there are a lot of grey areas, and that is where trouble lies. When life throws you a setback, take a deep breath, hold onto everything you've got and get through it. Be grateful for the smallest things, because even those don't always exist for others. You were designed to outlast any setback that is thrown your way. You can choose to grow and learn from it. You were created to be strong for this very moment, you don't have a choice but to get through it. You can and you will. I know things may look near impossible and I know you can't see a way out, but I encourage you to keep moving. Trust in what you know and keep moving. Build yourself up with self-love and positivity while pausing before you keep moving. Even though it may look like the storm won't pass this time, doesn't mean you have to stay there and wait, get up and keep moving. Because you will come out on top for yourself. Difficulties are put in your way to test your resilience and if you believe in your strength, there is nothing that can overcome you.

Day 12 – Mistakes are meant for growth not regret

Every decision that you have made up to this point, including the decision to purchase this book, has a significant role to play. Many times, we believe that our mistakes, due to our poor decisions, are things we should regret. There's a difference between saying it was a mistake and you learnt from it and saying it was a mistake and you regret it. Learning is our way of growing, and mistakes are part of it. No-one is perfect and I certainly don't want you to think that you have to be either. Because we all make mistakes and rightfully so. Without trial and error, the world that we know today wouldn't exist. So, I encourage you to own your mistakes, acknowledge them, understand them and accept them. This shows growth. Always remember that mistakes are there so you can learn from them and never make the same mistake again. If you continue to make the same mistakes, then you have not learnt and grown. For example, you left a pot of food cooking on high for forty-five minutes instead of thirty minutes, and the food at the bottom of the pot burnt. If you keep leaving the heat on for longer than thirty minutes, you will continue to burn the food. However, if you choose to learn from that experience, you will gain understanding and awareness that things need to be monitored and kept in balance at all time. Something as simple as that adds to your mental growth and it will forever remain as a vital lesson learnt. Adopt this into your life and will always grow from your experiences.

1. Think of all the mistakes you've made that you regret. Write them down, especially if it is something you don't want to remember or attempted to block out. Triggers for example.
2. Next to each regret, write down the reason. Why do you regret it? There is no wrong answer.
3. Write down whether or not that reason is still in your life, next to the why. Yes or no.
4. Take a different colour pen and put a line through the mistake/regret if your answer is no.
5. Now highlight the ones marked yes.

Notice how you feel about the ones scratched out. Since there is a definite line through it, it doesn't hold the same value anymore, right? Your regret now shifted to you. When you start holding yourself responsible of the things you regret, you open the door to growth.

Example; I regret dating ***inserts name here*** because they were a narcissist. No, they are no longer in my life.
~~I regret dating ***inserts name here*** because they were a narcissist. No, they are no longer in my life.~~
Now change the sentence to – I regret dating ***inserts name here*** because I allowed it to continue. There were signs and red flags, I just couldn't see them.

Looking at it from this point of view allows you to let go of the past and learn from it. Letting go is not always easy. Too often we blame others for our mistakes, when really all we should be doing is embracing the lesson that was taught in that scenario. The moment you take the person or thing out of the reason for regret, it changes your perspective. Living with regret is like walking around with gum stuck to your shoe. You know it's there and every time you try to remove it with a stick, it just gets stickier or you simply cannot remove it.

Journal Notes

___

___

___

___

___

___

___

___

___

___

___

Day 13 – Lessons learnt

The lessons you learn today, could teach someone tomorrow. Be fully aware of the individuals that admire you and have an appetite to learn from you and your success or experiences. We are meant to teach one another about what we know so that we may all evolve in this life. This is the very essence of our existence. Therefore, acknowledgments encourage growth. Never forget your purpose, even if it is not clear to you as yet. And always remember what you're going through right now, is for the lessons you have to teach tomorrow. Everyone is on a different level of consciousness.

Every encounter I have had the pleasure of experiencing has taught me two things; the love I have for people and the love I have to heal. What I also learnt through my journey is that you don't have to be close to someone or involved with someone to love them. Understanding their position in your life is key to how you will help them or how they will help you.

Draw up an appreciation post for everyone whom you appreciate, love and respect. This does not have to be broadcasted; it can be a private thing for you to keep.

Journal Notes

Day 14 – Surround yourself with success

It has been said that in order to be successful, you should surround yourself with successful people or people with similar mindsets. Do this even with individuals you aspire to reach and eventually surpass. Always remember, if you are the smartest person in the room, then you are in the wrong room.

If it is success that you seek, start with believing in yourself first. Self-belief is the first step to condition others to believe in you. You are your own competition and do not need to seek approval from anyone but yourself. I have heard the saying "you cannot expect someone to love you if you do not love yourself first". This may be considered has the hardest thing to do, but I assure you it is possible. Success comes from doing. And since you are alive and well, it would be an easy task to follow through.

Start with something simple.

1. What is the one thing you believe, without a doubt, about yourself?
2. What are you good at doing?
3. What do you love doing?
4. What would you like to start doing?

Understanding your level of capabilities is one step closer to success. It doesn't matter what that may look like to you, it is what you desire. Success is measured by assets, but not all success should be considered as wealth. Success could also be your state of mind, your health, your family. In some African cultures, if a man has a lot of children, he is considered as rich. Regardless of whether or not he can afford them, he will still be considered richer than a man without children. Whatever you consider as a measurement of success in your life, work towards that. It is about you and your journey.

Journal Notes

Day 15 – Dreams

Growing up I never really had one focused dream. All I knew is that I wanted to help people as my life's purpose. During the course of my journey, I obtained a few qualifications, none of which is my profession. At the time I believed this was the way for me to help people and live out my purpose. I was mistaken and very unfulfilled. And so, I decided to focus on what I would like to do for myself. The reason for this is because I would rather be doing something that makes me happy instead of something that drains me. When you are happy with your life, it is only then that you can truly live in your purpose. Your personal joy adds to your gift, and it will open the doors to your dreams. Which will ultimately lead to your personal vision of success.

This is not just about dreaming; it is about transforming your dreams into reality. If you do not take action towards achieving your dreams, you will regret it in time. It is not enough to just have a dream; you have to believe in that dream and believe in yourself too. When you know you can do it, you will do it. And that's the difference between you and dreamers. You are going to achieve great things because you are great and you believe it. The road to success may not be easy, but once you have reached the top, you will realize it was all worth it. Never stop dreaming if you plan on achieving those dreams. Never live a life filled with "What if" moments.

List all the dreams you've ever had since you can remember.

Now indicate which ones you can turn into a reality.

Do it.

Journal Notes

Day 16 – Acknowledge small victories

Imagine you are playing at the beach and your aim is to build a sand castle. That is your end goal. First you need to find the correct sand on the beach. Dry sand, which is closer to where you parked your car. Or wet sand, which is closer to the shore? Once you have decided, pick a spot on the beach. As small or insignificant as these few steps may seem, if not done correctly it could cost you your entire sand castle. A fully thought-out plan is far better than a complicated idea. Once you have successfully built your sand castle, be proud of it and acknowledge your small achievements along the way. Only you know and understand what it took to get to your end goal. More importantly only you experienced the frustrations along the way, and what it took to get through it. So, take a moment and appreciate your resolve and determination to achieve success. Apply this to your daily life and watch how different your day turns out.

Wake up tomorrow with an end goal in mind. It doesn't matter what it is. It could be to finish a task before the deadline at work. Or grocery shopping after work, knowing you might have little to no energy for it. One end goal is all you need for tomorrow.

Day 17 – What happens when you fail?

We can all admit that life is a series of dos and don'ts. There are certain things you do and certain things you don't. For example; do aim high no matter the risk and don't give up, no matter how hard. Because life will throw a curveball at you, and sometimes at every turn. You may dodge a few but if you get knocked down by one, remember to not let it keep you down. You have to get back up. Dust off your bruises (you may need them later), fix your outfit and carry on moving. Whatever you do, do not give up. You never know how close you really are. For example; the average safe diving depth is between 18-20 meters. More than twenty meters is known as deep sea diving. When a diver goes beyond twenty meters deep, they will start to experience a lot of internal pressure around the ears and chest. Making it nearly impossible to breathe, let alone continue swimming. And most divers give the signal to go back up the deeper they dive. Without realizing that they are literally one meter away from the bottom of the ocean.

Before you consider giving up, first take a moment to see how far you have come. Because sometimes, no matter how unbearable it becomes, you may only be one step away from achieving your goals and living out your dreams.

Success is built on a road of failures. The more you fail, the better you will succeed. Every time you try something new and fail, you are still doing better than most people. And that makes you a success, a winner. Keep trying. Keep setting yourself up. Keep believing. Eventually that wall will break down and you will walk right into the success of your purpose.

You will land the dream job that is meant for you
You will close the deal that is meant for you
You will get the contract that is meant for you
You will be a mom or dad if it is meant for you

It's about taking ownership of your dreams. What is your dream? And how do you plan on living it out? This is a question many of us get to at some point in our lives, and some of us are clear about what our dreams are. But what use is a clear dream if you don't take ownership of it. Living your own dream is crucial to being true to yourself. It may have the support of many around you, but without truly investing your mind and emotions into owning your dream, your dream will always be just that... A DREAM.

Day 18 – Alone time

There is one thing I know for certain, without any doubts, is the importance of your alone time. What if I told you that alone time is not just about refreshing, but it is also an opportunity to love yourself and even problem solve what you may be going through? When people hear "alone time" there is a misconception that this had to take the form of meditation. Alone time could be taking a drive, or a walk, spending time away from family or spouse for the night or even just a few hours. Alone time is really an opportunity to love yourself and also reflect on where you are in your life, what your next steps are and just acknowledging that loving yourself is a great starting point. If you are stuck in a dead-end job or are really unhappy doing what you do for a living, then you are actually letting yourself down and no-one else. Take time to get to know you again, so that you may refocus your energy on something more positive and promising.

What do you actually want to do, if you are not already doing it?

Love what you do by doing what you love. You were created with talents like no other, and the skill to enhance those talents through learning and observation. You owe it to yourself to be happy, so why not start with your career. If you are stuck in a job that is hiding your talents, then you need to leave. It may take you five months or five years to leave, but if you want it bad enough, it will happen no matter how long you have to wait. Keep encouraging yourself to accept a future filled with possibilities and a future that doesn't require you to do something you hate.

Journal Notes

Day 19 – Who am I?

The choices we make in life define who we are as individuals, unless you allow society to define and box you. So, the question is, who do you see yourself as? A lion? The king of the beasts. A boss in your own right and a leader to many? Or do you see yourself as a little rabbit? Prey to all other predators. Scared and timid but quick to respond to danger. Always battling to survive no matter the circumstance. Or do you consider yourself to be a beautiful butterfly? Who started off as a caterpillar, then transitioned into a cocoon of wonder before breaking free as the butterfly that you always envisioned? And even though most days you feel small and insignificant, you are powerful enough to create and leave an impact.

This analogy was created to help you see yourself from a different lens. It doesn't matter what your answer is if this is how you want others to see you. What you do with it afterwards is what matters. If you want people to see you as a lion, then you will have to live up to that expectation. If you prefer to be unseen like the rabbit, that is what you will be if you believe it to be true. Your mind is a powerful thing and if used correctly, a tool that can make you unstoppable.

Now I ask you again, who are you?

Journal Notes

Day 20 – Spirituality

The topic of spirituality is feared, loved and hated all in one sentence. People have been given the freedom of choice when it comes to believing in a higher power or vibrational energies. The trick is to not force your beliefs onto others and allow them to experience life the way they would like to. Having a spiritual or religious belief system, gives us a sense of purpose and belonging. Living in a world filled with unanswered questions can be very daunting, that is why people search for a deeper meaning. If you are someone who is searching right now, perhaps meditation might help with this or even learning about other faiths and practices.

When we see the word "meditation", we may assume it to be an environment of complete silence, spiritual candles or quiet pipe music, while sitting in deep thought. The truth is that meditation could be merely deep thought about something happening in your life. All true meditation requires is complete focus and intent. If you are in a situation where you need to make a decision, be it life changing or not, the idea is to weigh the pros and cons, and then make the decision that is beneficial to your overall well-being. It is vital to reflect on your options before committing to any result. Do more research if need be. This is not an immediate process, and it is important to take your time when reflecting on options prior to decision making. To a certain degree this process may seem simple for some. However, to simplify the thoughts in your mind can be a mentally draining process. It can drain your energy. It is important to be patient and allow it to reveal itself to you. Whatever is meant for you, will happen for you. Remember to breathe.

Day 21 – Gratitude

Showing gratitude can be a mere "thank you" to someone, but how many of us really show gratitude for every single daily gift we receive? We are caught in the race of life and forget to be grateful for waking up, breathing, a shower and so on.

This is about acknowledging the gifts we receive and appreciating the little and big things in life. When we are appreciative of the gifts, we receive from life we start to live better. Simply count your blessings before you go to sleep at night. This does not have to be material things, because truth is, material things are not an example of blessings. Your good health is an example. Your husband or wife lying next to you is an example. Your child or children in the next room is an example. The business deal you just closed, the exam you just passed, the promotion you just received at work, and the approval for your home loan are examples of good blessings. Do not confuse blessings with material things, because material things are only the by-product of those blessings. Be thankful for the door that opened and the opportunity that presented itself through that opened door. Once you recognise the root of your blessings, your gratitude will transform to new heights, leaving you with a better life lived.

Take some time and write down everything you are grateful for today.

Journal Notes

Final thoughts

Congratulations! You have taken the first step to ensure a happier you. Taking control of your life is the best decision you could have made for yourself. Understanding who you are, a little every day goes a long way. Even though this is just the beginning, your new founded confidence will help you make this journey worthwhile.

Enjoy the new you!

Love and light
Sunil
#SUNNYMOTIV

***

www.ingramcontent.com/pod-product-compliance
Ingram Content Group UK Ltd.
Pitfield, Milton Keynes, MK11 3LW, UK
UKHW020223250726
13967UKWH00001B/159